THE PIRATE WHO SAVED CHRISTMAS

A play by

L. Henry Dowell

BLACK BOX THEATRE PUBLISHING

Copyright © 2016 by L. Henry Dowell
ALL RIGHTS RESERVED

CAUTION: Professionals and amateurs are hereby warned that

The Pirate Who Save Christmas

is subject to a royalty. It is fully protected under the copyright laws of the
United States of America, the British Commonwealth, including Canada,
and all other countries of the Copyright Union.
All rights, including professional, amateur, motion
picture, recitation, lecturing, public reading, radio broadcasting,
television and the rights of translation into foreign languages
are strictly reserved. The right to photocopy scripts or videotape
performances can be granted only by the author. In some cases,
the author may choose to allow this, provided permission has
been requested prior to the production. No alterations, deletions
or substitutions may be made to the work without the
written permission of the author.

All publicity material must contain the author's name,
as the sole author of the work.

By producing this play you give the author and

BLACK BOX THEATRE PUBLISHING

the right to use any publicity material
including pictures, programs and posters generated
from the production.

To order additional copies of the script, or
to request performance rights, please contact us at
wwwblackboxtheatrepublishing.com

ISBN 978-1946613004

Printed in the United States of America.

CAST

Narrator
Nicholas The Horrible
Dasher
Dancer
Prancer
Vixen
Comet
Cupid
Donner
Mortimer
Zombie Pirate
Stealthy Ninja
Strange Being
Weird Sea Creature
Spooky Vampire
Pushy Encyclopedia Salesman
Overbearing Girl Scout
Mutant Cheerleader
Evil Robot
Sgt. Releve
Captain Capeman
Cyborg Bear
Horsey
Go-Bot
Bleeping Betty
Sir Tidybowl
Tickle Me Fuzzball
The Pirate Queen
Lady Pirates (Optional)

THE PIRATE WHO SAVED CHRISTMAS

MUSIC: An old, instrumental Christmas Carol plays.

LIGHTS: Rise on the deck of a pirate ship. NARRATOR enters.

NARRATOR
If you are the sort who loves a good pirate tale then you have come to the right place. If you are the kind of person who enjoys stories of swashbuckling knavery then sit back and listen to what I have to tell you, lads and lassies. You have, no doubt, heard tell of Black Beard and Blue Beard and Red Beard and Gray Beard. Terrible cutthroats, one and all. But there was once a pirate so awful, so mean and terrible that he made all of those other pirates look like kindergarten teachers. They called him Nicholas the Horrible because let's face it, he was.

> NICHOLAS enters, huge and red and terrifying with a long white beard.

NICHOLAS
You better believe it! Yo-ho-ho-ho-ho-ho!!!

NARRATOR
His laugh was so terrifying, it would make his enemies surrender without a fight.

CAST
(Offstage.)
We surrender!

NARRATOR
See what I mean? Nicholas only wanted one thing out of life.

NICHOLAS
Fame and fortune! Yo-ho-ho-ho-ho-ho!

NARRATOR
That's two things.

NICHOLAS gives HIM a dirty look.

NARRATOR
He was so tough, he'd eat a pound of nails for breakfast and wash them down with a keg of rum.

NICHOLAS belches loudly.

NICHOLAS
That's good stuff!

NARRATOR
For lunch he'd eat half a shark. Wait…only half?

NICHOLAS
I'm watching me figure!

NARRATOR
…and he'd wash that down with another keg of rum.

NICHOLAS belches again.

NICHOLAS
Like I said, good stuff!

NARRATOR
And for his supper he'd eat the other half of the shark, a few more nails, a keg of rum and….a Cream Brule?

NICHOLAS
A pirate cannot live by rum alone…yo ho!

NARRATOR
Speaking of pirates, his crew consisted of some of the worst misfits ever to sail the seven seas. The story of how Nicholas assembled them was fascinating but due to time constraints, that story will have to wait till another day. First, there was Dasher the Quick!

> DASHER enters quickly, strikes pose. HE speaks very fast.

DASHER
That'srightI'mfast,realfast!Wannamakesomethingofit?

NARRATOR
Dancer the Nimble!

> DANCER enters dancing around the stage, finally bowing and striking a pose.

DANCER
I studied with Bob Fosse, you know.

NARRATOR
Prancer the…Prancer…I guess.

> PRANCER enters, dressed elegantly, speaking in an aloof accent.

PRANCER
Someone has to provide a touch of class to these ruffians.

DANCER
Who's he calling a ruffian?

DASHER
What'saruffian?

NARRATOR
Vixen the Lady Pirate!

VIXEN enters, strikes pose.

VIXEN
Look. I know you probably think I'm some sort of "bad girl" because my name is Vixen but it couldn't be farther from the truth. I'm a very nice person. Take my word for it.
> (OTHER PIRATES laugh. SHE shoots THEM a look.)

Hey!
> (THEY shut up fast.)

NARRATOR
Comet the Navigator!

> COMET enters with telescope, strikes pose, pointing to the stars.

COMET
Second star to the right and straight on till morning, Captain!

> PIRATES look confused.

NICHOLAS
We're going the other direction, Mr. Comet.

COMET
Oh!
> (Points the other direction.)

In that case…third star to the left and straight on till midnight, Captain!

NARRATOR
Cupid the Archer!
> (CUPID enters with bow and strikes a pose.)

Archer? Really? You couldn't come up with anything more creative than that?

CUPID
I'm not just an archer.

NARATOR

No?

CUPID

Absolutely not! I'm also the ship's resident matchmaker.

NARRATOR

Of course you are.

CUPID

What are you? A Pisces? You seem like a Pisces. Do you like sushi?

NARRATOR

Moving along…the First Mate, Donner.
> (DONNER enters, strikes pose to the left of NICHOLAS.)

He was Nicholas's right hand man.

> DONNER notices HE'S on the wrong side of NICHOLAS and quickly moves to the right side.

DONNER

I'm always getting confused on that. Is it the actor's right or the audience's right? And what if you're facing upstage? I mean, I went to drama school but some theories just don't always make sense, you know, when you have to practically apply them.

NICHOLAS

Mr. Donner!

DONNER

Yes, Captain?

NICHOLAS

Quit yer yappin!

DONNER
(Saluting.)
Aye aye, Captain!

NARRATOR
Let's see...who am I forgetting? Dasher, Dancer, Prancer, Vixen, Comet, Cupid, Donner and....oh yes, of course! How could I forget...Mortimer. Mortimer the Accountant!

> MORTIMER enters. A nerdy pirate wearing glasses and carrying a stack of books. HE strikes a pose...sort of.

MORTIMER
A pirate ship is a business after all and a business must keep good records if it's going to be successful. Heavens! What in the world would the Captain do if we were to get audited?

> PIRATES agree.

NARRATOR
And that was Nicholas's crew and a motley crew they were, too.

NICHOLAS
Really? They look more like ZZ Top to me! Yo-ho-ho-ho-ho-ho!

PIRATES
Yo-ho-ho-ho-ho-ho!

NARRATOR
That's an old joke.

NICHOLAS
What did you say, Mr. Narrator?

NARRATOR
(Intimidated.)
Nothing, Captain!

NICHOLAS
That's what I thought you said.

NARRATOR
Moving on…their ship was an imposing vessel known throughout the seafaring world by its not so subtle name, The Big Red Slayer!

NICHOLAS
Who ever heard of a subtle pirate, anyway?

PIRATES agree.

NARRATOR
Throughout the years, the crew had faced many, many adversaries including…Zombie Pirates!

> ZOMBIE PIRATE enters, strikes an attack pose.

ZOMBIE PIRATE
Brains! Brains! Brains!

NARRATOR
You're in the wrong place for that, matey.

NICHOLAS
(PIRATES also growling.)
What did you say?

NARRATOR
Moving along…Stealthy Ninjas!
(STEALTHY NINJA enters and strikes a pose. Stays silent.)
The strong, silent type, huh?

STEALTHY NINJA
That's me!
> (EVERYONE looks at HIM.)

Oops!

NARRATOR
Then the crew faced off against a horde of Spooky Vampires!
> (Pause. CAST looks around.)

Hello? I said…then the crew faced off against a horde of Spooky Vampires!
> (Pause.)

I said, Spooky Vampires!!!

DASHER
Look!
> (Points towards sky above audience.)

A vampire bat!

> ALL run around stage screaming. SPOOKY VAMPIRE enters among the chaos.

SPOOKY VAMPIRE
What's all the fuss about?

DASHER
It'savampireandhe'sgoingtobiteournecksandsuckourblood!

VAMPIRE
A vampire? How frightening!

DANCER
I did not spend four years at Julliard for this!

NICHOLAS
(Loud and booming.)
STOP!!!
(THEY do.)
NOW GET BACK IN PLACES!
(THEY do.)
Mr. Narrator. Would you like to continue?

NARRATOR
Certainly, Captain. I was just about to get to the denizens of the deep, the Weird Sea Creatures!

> WEIRD SEA CREATURE enters. HE has a large octopus head.

PRANCER
Weird is right. What are you supposed to be?

WEIRD SEA CREATURE
I am Davey Jones! Master of the Underworld! Captain of the Dead! Keeper of Davy Jones' Locker!

NICHOLAS
What brings ye to the surface world?

WEIRD SEA CREATURE
(Breaking character. A bit wimpy.)
I lost my combination.

> HE shrugs to the audience and strikes a formidable pose.

NARRATOR
(Shrugging to audience.)
There was also an adventure where the crew faced Strange Beings from another planet!

> STRANGE BEING enters. HE steps to center stage and points at the audience.

STRANGE BEING
Take me to your leader.

> CAST points at NICHOLAS, who crosses to the STRANGE BEING.

NICHOLAS
All right. I am the captain of this ship. You desire to parley, I assume?

STRANGE BEING
Elliot?

NICHOLAS
What did you say?

STRANGE BEING
Elliot?

NICHOLAS
No. My name is not Elliot. My name is Nicholas. Nicholas the Horrible. I am the captain of this ship!

STRANGE BEING
Phone home?

NICHOLAS
What?

STRANGE BEING
Phone home?

NICHOLAS
Does anyone know what he's talking about?

VIXEN
It sounds like some kind of foreign language.

COMET
I think he's from beyond the stars!

CUPID
I think he's Italian!

DONNER
That's it! It must be! He's Italian!

PIRATES agree that HE must be Italian.

NARRATOR
(Looking at pocket watch.)
May we move this along?

NICHOLAS
What's your hurry, Mr. Narrator?

NARRATOR
If we're going to market this tale on the competition circuit or as an animated feature, it has to come in under a certain time.

MORTIMER
He's right, Captain. There are economic concerns that must be addressed!

NICHOLAS
What? You mean this might affect my booty?
(PIRATES laugh.)
Hey!
(THEY go silent.)
We've talked about this.

PIRATES
Sorry.

NICHOLAS
Mortimer?

MORTIMER
Oh yes, Captain. The profitability of this venture is certainly dependent on its marketability. There's no doubt about it, whatsoever!

NICHOLAS
In that case, Mr. Narrator, proceed with haste!

NARRATOR
Aye aye, Captain!
(To audience.)
The crew faced a fantastic array of adversaries as we've seen and many others… like Evil Robots, Mutant Cheerleaders, Pushy Encyclopedia Salesmen and Overbearing Girl Scouts!
(THEY enter quickly and strike poses.)
Wait…Overbearing Girl Scouts? You fought Girl Scouts? How overbearing could a Girl Scout be?

OVERBEARING GIRL SCOUT
Who wants to buy some cookies?

CAST runs around screaming in terror.

NICHOLAS
(Loud.)
STOP!!!

CAST
Sorry.

OVERBEARING GIRL SCOUT
Seriously though, does anyone want to buy any cookies?

CAST looks at HER in horror.

NARRATOR
Moving on…the crew of The Big Red Slayer had many adventures over the years and fought in many sword clanking battles…unfortunately, we don't have enough time to show you any of that…

NICHOLAS
Wait a minute! What do you mean, we don't have time to show them any of that?

NARRATOR
Captain, we've been over this.

NICHOLAS
(Drawing sword. Steps towards NARRATOR.)
Now you hear this! These pirates signed up to be in this here pirate show with certain…expectations. Am I right, pirate crew?
(PIRATES growl.)
And this here audience came to see this pirate show with certain expectations too. Am I right, audience?
(Audience growls.)
Now you better make with some pirate type action, real fast. Savvy?

NARRATOR
Savvy, Captain…but if we do this, we'll have to cut a scene from later in the show.

NICHOLAS
(Backs off.)
Which scene?

NARRATOR
Almost certainly your big romantic scene with the lady pirate you meet later. Can you live with that?

NICHOLAS
(Thinking. Looks at PIRATES.)
I'll have to.

NARRATOR
Which tale shall I tell them, Captain? There are so many. I mean, look at your collection of villains…it's enormous!
>(Suddenly realizing.)

Wait! I've got it!
>(Clears throat.)

The crew of The Big Red Slayer had many adventures over the years and fought in many sword clanking battles…BUT…none of those battles were any larger or more dramatic than the day…THEY WERE ATTACKED BY ALL THEIR ENEMIES AT THE SAME TIME!!!

>VILLAINS draw swords on PIRATES.

NICHOLAS
>(Looking at NARRATOR.)

You did good, lad. You did good.
>(Yelling.)

PIRATES ATTACK!!!

>SOUND: Battle Music. NOTE: The battle between this large group should be impressive. There's a lot to work with here. Make it as impressive as possible. When it's over, the MUSIC fades and the VILLAINS have been defeated and surrounded by the PIRATES.

DONNER
We've won the day, Captain!

>PIRATES cheer.

VIXEN
What do we do with these cads now that we've defeated them, Captain?

NICHOLAS
We're pirates! What do you think we do with our prisoners?
We make them walk the plank!

>   PIRATES cheer. THEY get a long plank
>   and extend it toward the audience.

DASHER
Whichoneshallwemakewalktheplankfirst?Tellme!Tellme!

NICHOLAS
Oh that's an easy question ye be asking, Mr. Dasher. We'll make the worst of the worst go first. The most vile, villainous creature we've ever faced will take the plunge into those shark infested waters!
> (HE points at the OVERBEARING GIRL
> SCOUT.)

The Overbearing Girl Scout!

>   PIRATES howl with approval. THEY lead
>   HER to the plank. SHE steps forward, then
>   suddenly stops.

OVERBEARING GIRL SCOUT
Are you sure you don't want to buy some cookies?

PIRATES
> (Chanting.)

Walk the plank! Walk the plank! Walk the plank!

OVERBEARING GIRL SCOUT
Okay. If you're sure.
> (SHE takes a step. Notices something in the
> water.)

Hey! What's that?

>   EVERYONE moves to the edge of the
>   ship/stage, looking out into the water.

DANCER
What are those things?

PUSHY ENCYCLOPEDIA SALESMAN
They look like toys!

PRANCER
Toys?

NICHOLAS
Indeed, they do look like toys.

MUTANT CHEERLEADER
Why would they be floating out here in the ocean?

TOYS
(From somewhere in the audience.)
Help us! Please! Someone! The water's cold! Etc!

EVIL ROBOT
They're calling for help!

COMET
What do you care? You're an evil robot!

EVIL ROBOT
And you are a pirate!

COMET
Touché.

CUPID
Captain? What should we do?

TOYS
Help us! Help us!

CUPID
Captain?

                    TOYS
Help us! Help us!

                    CUPID
CAPTAIN???

                    NICHOLAS
Oh, all right! Bring them aboard.

>   The PIRATES throw ropes over the side and
>   retrieve the TOYS. Once THEY are aboard
>   THEY line up. SGT. RELEVE steps
>   forward. A toy soldier on top and a ballerina
>   on bottom.

                    SGT. RELEVE
         (Saluting.)
My name is Sgt. Releve and I'd like to thank you for
rescuing me and these other toys, sir. Our boat crashed into
an iceberg and was destroyed.

                    NICHOLAS
Crashed into an iceberg? Really?

                    SGT. RELEVE
Yes, sir! Went straight to the bottom.

                    NICHOLAS
I find it hard to believe an iceberg could sink such a large
ship.

                    SGT. RELEVE
It happens more often than you think.

                    NICHOLAS
And why exactly were you sailing this far north? I can't
imagine what business a ship full of toys would have in these
cold waters.

SGT. RELEVE
We're outcasts, sir.

NICHOLAS
What?

SGT. RELEVE
Rejects. Imperfect. Defective. Misfits. That's what we are. As you can see, I'm half a soldier, half a ballerina.

NICHOLAS
I did notice that. I just assumed it was some new sort of new camouflage the military was trying out.

SGT. RELEVE
No, sir. The toymaker got mixed up and gave me the wrong bottom half. Or maybe he gave me the wrong top half. It's very confusing. I don't know if I'm supposed to attack the enemy or dance the Nutcracker for them.

NICHOLAS
What about the rest of your friends?

SGT. RELEVE
Introduce yourself to the captain, guys.

> CAPTAIN CAPEMAN steps forward, holding an incredibly long cape.

CAPTAIN CAPEMAN
Hi there. My name is Captain Capeman.

CAST
Hello, Captain Capeman.

CAPTAIN CAPEMAN
I am a superhero toy. I've got this neat costume and all except for this really, really, really, really, really, really, really long cape! And it's NOT at all like it is in the comic books and the cartoons, you know, with the cape flowing in the wind behind you. Most of the time there isn't any wind, you know what I mean? I end up having to carry this thing around with me. I've been thinking about getting a wheelbarrow to haul it around in. This thing is the worst trip hazard! That's all I'm saying.

> HE steps back as CYBORG BEAR steps forward. Half cuddly, half cold hearted robot.

CYBORG BEAR
They call me the Teddy 2000.

CAST
Hello, Teddy 2000.

CYBORG BEAR
I am a cute, fuzzy plaything on the outside but I have a metal endoskeleton on the inside. I'm a cybernetic weapon of total destruction and I've been sent here from the future to destroy John Conner before he can become the leader of the resistance. Bwah-ha-ha-ha-ha!

> EVERYONE looks at EACH OTHER.

NICHOLAS
Who is this John Conner you speak of?

CYBORG BEAR
(Pause.)
Hasta la vista, baby!

> HE steps back in line as HORSEY steps forward.

HORSEY
Hi there. I am a unicorn.

CAST
Hello, Unicorn.

NICHOLAS
Unicorn?

HORSEY
That's right.

NICHOLAS
Then where's your horn?

HORSEY
I never received one.

NICHOLAS
Maybe you're a horse.

HORSEY
Nope.

NICHOLAS
What's your name?

HORSEY
Horsey.

NICHOLAS
Your name is Horsey?

HORSEY
That is correct.

NICHOLAS
But you aren't a horse?

HORSEY
Nope. Just a coincidence.

NICHOLAS
Mate, I don't want to argue with you but I think there's a pretty good chance that you are a horse.

HORSEY
Unicorn.

NICHOLAS
Next!
>   (HORSEY steps back in line as GO-BOT steps forward. HE'S a transforming robot with low self esteem.)

And you are?

GO-BOT
I am Go-Bot, sir.

CAST
Hello, Go-Bot.

NICHOLAS
And what kind of toy are you?

GO-BOT
I am a Go-Bot, sir.

NICHOLAS
And what is your defect?

GO-BOT
I am a Go-Bot, sir.

>   HE steps back in line as BLEEPING BETTY steps forth. SHE is a baby doll in a pretty dress.

NICHOLAS

Well! Aren't you the cutest baby doll in the whole wide world! I bet some little girl would love to have you for a plaything. What's your name, sweetheart?
>   (When SHE opens HER mouth to speak it is replaced with SOUND: Censored bleep. NICHOLAS is shocked.)

What did you say?
>   (Bleep.)

That's what I thought you said!
>   (Bleep, bleep bleep.)

Where did you learn to talk like that?
>   (Bleep.)

She did not! In fact I doubt you have ever even met my mother!
>   (Bleep, bleep.)

She does not!
>   (Bleep, bleep, bleep, bleep.)

Yes, I may be a bit on the portly side but that doesn't mean you can go around calling me names!
>   (Bleep, bleep, bleeeeeeeeep.)

Stop that! You're making the pirates blush!
>   (Bleep, bleep, bleep, bleep, bleep.)

Oh yeah? Well I was wrong! You are not the cutest baby doll in the whole wide world!
>   (SHE cries.)

Oh no. Don't do that. Don't start crying.

>   SGT RELEVE steps forward to console HER.

SGT. RELEVE

Don't let her vocabulary fool you, sir. She's really very sensitive.

NICHOLAS
I see.
>(To PIRATES.)

I'll explain what some of those words mean to you pirates, later.
>(Resuming.)

Who's next?

> SIR TIDYBOWL steps forward. A knight
> in an apron with a plunger

SIR TIDYBOWL
That would be me, Your Majesty!

NICHOLAS
Your Majesty? I like that. I can plainly see that you are a knight but what is your name?

SIR TIDYBOWL
I am known far and wide as Sir Tidybowl, Your Majesty.

CAST
Hello, Sir Tidybowl.

NICHOLAS
You seem to be well adjusted, Sir Tidybowl. How did you happen to end up on the ship with these others?

SIR TIDYBOWL
Thank you for the compliment, Your Majesty. I like to think I do my best. In answer to your question, you may have noticed that instead of a sword and shield, the toymaker decided to accessorize me with an apron and a toilet plunger.

NICHOLAS
Unusual weapons for a knight.

SIR TIDYBOWL

Indeed. And also unusual for a toy knight, I'm afraid. You see, very few boys want to play with an action figure outfitted for latrine duty.

NICHOLAS

I suppose that makes sense.

SIR TIDYBOWL

It's a dirty job but some toy has to do it!

> HE steps back in line as TICKLE ME FUZZBALL steps forward. A furry red monster.

NICHOLAS

And you are?

> TICKLE ME FUZZBALL starts laughing.

TICKLE ME FUZZBALL

That tickles!

> HE continues to laugh.

NICHOLAS

I don't understand what's so funny.

TICKLE ME FUZZBALL

That's funny!

NICHOLAS

I don't see…

TICKLE ME FUZZBALL

That tickles!

NICHOLAS

But…

TICKLE ME FUZZBALL

That tickles!

NICHOLAS

Throw him overboard!

TICKLE ME FUZZBALL

That tickles!

SGT. RELEVE

Captain! Please?

NICHOLAS

Oh, never mind.

SGT. RELEVE

He has an off switch.

> HE flips a switch on the back of TICKLE ME FUZZBALL'S head.

TICKLE ME FUZZBALL

That…

> TICKLE ME FUZZBALL goes limp.

NICHOLAS

That's a useful thing to know.
(PIRATES agree.)
Now that we know who ye be, the question is where were you headed when ye hit that iceberg?

SGT. RELEVE

The Island of Imperfect Playthings.

NICHOLAS

Never heard of it.

> COMET takes map out and looks at it.

COMET
I don't see any sign of an island by that name in these waters, Captain.

SGT. RELEVE
I'm not surprised. Very few people know of its existence. It's where toymakers send all of their "mistakes". That's why we were going there. Captain…do you think you could take us to the island? We would be ever so grateful!

TOYS agree.

NICHOLAS
I don't know. Delivering toys really isn't what we do. We're more of the pilfering and pillaging type. Am I right, Pirates?

PIRATES agree.

SGT. RELEVE
Did I mention our island is run by a group of beautiful lady pirates?

NICHOLAS
On second thought, delivering toys sounds like a nice change of pace. Don't you agree, Pirates?
    (PIRATES agree, enthusiastically.)
Besides, we need a place to drop off these villains. Do they have room on that island for a few extra misfits?

SGT. RELEVE
The more the merrier!

NICHOLAS
Sail on, me hearties!

ALL face forward.

NARRATOR
And on they did sail, this crew of pirates, villains and toys in search of the Island of Imperfect Playthings...when suddenly a horrible winter storm blew in! The worst storm in a century!

> SOUND: Wind howls. The CAST moves from side to side to indicate the tossing of the ship. FX: Heavy fog if possible.

PRANCER
Captain! Where did this storm come from?

NICHOLAS
From Mr. Dramatic over here!
(Pointing at NARRATOR.)

NARRATOR
The temperature dropped 40 degrees. Visibility was at zero. No one could see their hand in front of their face.

> ALL put THEIR hands in front of THEIR faces, shrug.

VIXEN
We're going to freeze to death before we get to this island, Captain.

> SOUND: Storm subsides. NICHOLAS thinks for a minute and then begins to sing. NOTE: Pick any carol but it's suggested to use something old and slow. The CAST joins in.

NARRATOR
And so it was on this Christmas Eve, that this rag tag crew found common ground...at least, until this happened...

> SOUND: Enormous crash. The CAST falls

>   all over THEMSELVES.

>   NICHOLAS
> Shiver me timbers! What did we hit?

>   SGT. RELEVE
> I bet it was an iceberg!

>   NICHOLAS
> Will you stop with that iceberg business!

>   SGT. RELEVE
> Just saying.

>   DONNER
> I think we've run aground, Captain!

>   NICHOLAS
> Run aground? My insurance premiums will go through the roof!

>   MORTIMER
> Not good. Not good.

>   DANCER
> Look!
>   (Pointing in the distance.)
> Something is coming this way!

>   DASHER
> Not something…SOMEONE!

>   CUPID
> IT'S A WOMAN!!!

>   CAST comb THEIR hair, check THEIR
>   breath, etc. PIRATE QUEEN enters. SHE'S
>   beautiful, in a roguish sort of way. NOTE:
>   Extra LADY PIRATES can be added.

PIRATE QUEEN
Who is the captain of this ship?

NICHOLAS
I'm the captain! And who might ye be?

THEY circle EACH OTHER.

PIRATE QUEEN
I am the queen of this island!

NICHOLAS
A pirate queen?

PIRATE QUEEN
And what of it?

NICHOLAS
I've never heard of such.

PIRATE QUEEN
Then listen to this!

SHE draws HER sword. HE does the same.
THEY have an incredible battle.

NICHOLAS
(During the fight. Impressed.)
Magnificent!

PIRATE QUEEN
You aren't so bad yourself!

NICHOLAS
You know, I gave up a romantic scene with you to get more sword fighting in the show.

PIRATE QUEEN
What are you talking about? This is a romantic scene!

> The fight intensifies. Finally, SHE disarms HIM. CAST is shocked.

NICHOLAS
Impossible! I've never been bested by any man!

PIRATE QUEEN
Then your record remains intact, pirate, for I am no man! Now tell me, what brings you to The Island of Imperfect Playthings?

NICHOLAS
We found some of your people floating in the water and brought them here as an act of charity.

CUPID
And to see the lady pirates!

PIRATE QUEEN
I see. That makes more sense. You didn't strike me as the toy delivery type. Nor the charitable type for that matter.

NICHOLAS
You'd be surprised, Pirate Queen.

PIRATE QUEEN
Is that a fact? Then perhaps you'd like to help us?

NICHOLAS
Help you?

PIRATE QUEEN
The toys who come to this island may be imperfect but they want the same things as any other toy. A child to love and play with them and give them a home.

NICHOLAS
I'm afraid I don't follow.

PIRATE QUEEN
My crew of lady pirates and I used to rescue toys from this island ourselves and take then to children across the world. That is, until we hit an iceberg and our ship was sunk.

CAST looks at SGT. RELEVE.

SGT. RELEVE
I told you so.

NICHOLAS
What are you saying?

PIRATE QUEEN
I want you to take the toys on this island and find them children who will love them for who they are. Imperfections and all.

DONNER
Captain? We're the pilfering and pillaging types, remember?

NICHOLAS
That's right, Mr. Donner. Thank you.
(To PIRATE QUEEN.)
You said it yourself, I don't seem like the toy delivery type.

PIRATE QUEEN
But you could be! You have the one element absolutely essential to be successful in the toy delivery business.

NICHOLAS
And what's that?

PIRATE QUEEN
A means of transportation.

CAST agrees.

NICHOLAS
And what does this job pay?

PIRATE QUEEN
The love and admiration of little children worldwide.

NICHOLAS
Hard to buy rum with that. I think I'll pass.

PIRATE QUEEN
What about immortality?

NICHOLAS
What did you say?

PIRATE QUEEN
Immortality. Imagine the legends and tales and songs that would arise from someone spreading so much good cheer around the world. That person, whoever it was, would achieve a glorious fame like no other.

NICHOLAS
Aye, lass. That he would.

DONNER
Pilfer and pillage, Captain. Pilfer and pillage.

NICHOLAS
And where has pilfering and pillaging gotten us? Abject poverty! Why, I'd say we make less money than a piddling stage actor!

MORTIMER
It's true. We're very poor.

NICHOLAS
(To PIRATE QUEEN.)
But we're grounded. How do you expect to remedy that?

PIRATE QUEEN
We have a toy tug boat. He'll pull you back out to sea.

NICHOLAS
What do you say, Crew? Are ye interested in giving up your lives of piracy to deliver toys to the kiddies in The Big Red Slayer, here?

PIRATES grunt and grown, unhappily.

PIRATE QUEEN
When you're finished delivering toys you could come back here and live with me and my lady pirates. How about that?

PIRATES agree enthusiastically.

NICHOLAS
They seem to like that idea.

PIRATE QUEEN
And you? Do you like the idea?

NICHOLAS
I do. What about our prisoners? What shall we do with them?

PIRATE QUEEN
Maybe they'd like to stay here as well. Live on the island and help us. There are new toys arriving all the time.

NICHOLAS
What say you, villains? Would you like to live on this island among the misfits?

OVERBEARING GIRL SCOUT steps forward.

OVERBEARING GIRL SCOUT
I think that would be nice. We are misfits ourselves, after all.

NICHOLAS
We're all misfits here, little girl.

SHE hugs HIM.

OVERBEARING GIRL SCOUT
How about some cookies, fellow misfit?

NICHOLAS
Fine! I'll buy some cookies! Which reminds me...
(To PIRATE QUEEN.)
What about the naughty children? The ones who are most likely to grow up and become pirates or villains like us. Do we give them toys as well?

PIRATE QUEEN
Perhaps you could leave them some sort of reminder in their stockings that they need to change their ways. Something like...a lump of coal, perhaps.

MORTIMER
Coal? Are you out of your mind? Do you know how expensive coal is? No, that's out of the question.

NICHOLAS
You heard the accountant. We'll just have to do something else to discourage the naughty children.
(Sudden realization.)
Wait! I know! We'll make them walk the plank! Every last naughty one of them! Yo-ho-ho-ho-ho-ho!!!

ALL
Yo-ho-ho-ho-ho-ho!!!

NARRATOR
And so it came to pass, the crew of The Big Red Slayer began loading the ship with toys and...oh no!

NICHOLAS
What do you mean, oh no?

NARRATOR
The winter storm had gotten worse.
> (SOUND: Wind howls. Fog.)

Much worse.
> (SOUND: Louder wind. More fog.)

There was no way the crew would be able to set out that night.

CAST sighs in disappointment.

NICHOLAS
Surely there's something we can do. Mr. Comet?

COMET
I'm sorry, Captain. Visibility is zero. We'll just have to wait till the storm passes.

NICHOLAS
How long will that be?

COMET
Uh…I don't know…Spring, maybe.

CAST
Spring???

NARRATOR
Wait! I have an idea!

NICHOLAS
Don't keep us in the dark, man! What is it?

NARRATOR
I have a lantern. A very special lantern that shines so bright it can cut through any storm. Any fog. No matter how thick.

HE holds up a large, intensely bright, red lantern.

NICHOLAS
I say! That is the brightest lantern I have ever seen. What powers it?

NARRATOR
Magic, Captain. Christmas magic.

NICHOLAS
You've done well, Mr. Narrator…say, I don't think I know your real name. I've always called you Mr. Narrator. What is it?

NARRATOR
It's Rudolph, sir. My name is Rudolph.

NICHOLAS
Very well then. Mr. Rudolph, with your lamp so bright won't you guide The Slayer tonight?

NARRATOR
It would be my distinct honor, Captain.

CAST cheers.

NICHOLAS
Let's get this ship loaded up then and be on our way! Come on you pirates! Get to work!

PIRATES
Aye, aye Captain!
(THEY hustle about.)

NICHOLAS
You too, you villains!

VILLAINS
Aye, aye Captain!
> (THEY hustle about.)

NICHOLAS
There are kids waiting on those toys! Yo-ho-ho-ho-ho-ho!

NARRATOR
And so it came to pass, the crew of The Big Red Slayer began loading the ship with toys and playthings to deliver to boys and girls all over the world. Of course, it took Nicholas and his crew eight months to get everything delivered but deliver it they did, eventually making their way back to the North Pole and The Island of Imperfect Playthings. He made a second delivery the very next Christmas and this time it only took him half as long. Year after year, always at Christmas, Nicholas would set out from the North Pole with his toys until he had become so good at the job he could complete it in one night. Of course, he had discovered much faster means of transportation by then. Nicholas the Horrible did achieve great fame as he had set out to do but not for being an ill tempered pirate. Instead, he became a symbol synonymous with the season itself. A symbol of generosity, good will and love, known the world over…as Santa Claus!

> The CAST has formed a large tableau and sing a happy carol with a little pirate flair.

THE END

Thank you for purchasing and reading this play. If you enjoyed it, we'd appreciate a review on Amazon.com.

On the following pages you will find a selection of other plays from the Black Box Theatre Publishing Company catalog presented for you at no additional cost.

Enjoy!!!

www.blackboxtheatrepublishing.com

"Poop Happens!" in this family friendly cowboy comedy!

So, Who Was That Masked Guy Anyway? is the story of Ernie, the grandson of the original Masked Cowboy, a lawman who fought for truth, justice and the cowboy way in the old west. Now that Grandpa is getting on in years he's looking for someone to carry on for him. The only problem? Ernie doesn't know anything about being a cowboy. He's never seen a real cow, he's allergic to milk and to tell the truth he doesn't know one end of a horse from another...but beware, before it's all over, the poop is sure to hit the fans!

Cast Size: 21 Flexible M-F Roles Doubling Possible.

Royalties: $50.00 per performance.

Running Time: Approximately 90 minutes.

WANTED: SANTA CLAUS is the story of what happens when a group of department store moguls decide to replace Santa Claus with the shiny new "KRINGLE 3000", codenamed...ROBO-SANTA! Now it's up to Santa's elves to save the day! But Santa's in no shape to take on his stainless steel counterpart! He'll have to train for his big comeback. Enter Mickey, one of the toughest elves of all time! He'll get Santa ready for the big showdown! But it's going to mean reaching deep down inside to find "the eye of the reindeer"!

Cast Size 23 Flexible M-F Roles Doubling Possible.

Royalties: $50.00 per performance.

Running Time: Approximately 90 Minutes.

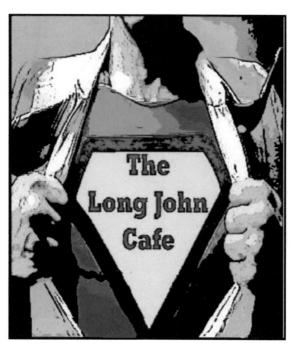

At the edge of the universe sits The Long John Cafe. A place where the average guy and the average "Super" guy can sit and have a cup of coffee and just be themselves...or, someone else if that's what they want. The cafe is populated by iconic figures of the 20th Century, including cowboys, hippies, super heroes and movie stars. They've come to celebrate the end of the old Century and the beginning of tomorrow! That is, if they make it through the night! It seems the evil Dr. McNastiman has other plans for our heroes. Like their total destruction!

Cast Size: 17 9M 8F.

Royalties: $50.00 per performance.

Running Time: Approximately 90 Minutes.

Jacklyn Sparrow and the Lady Pirates of the Caribbean is our brand new swashbuckling pirate parody complete with bloodthirsty buccaneers in massive sword clanking battle scenes!! A giant wise cracking parrot named Polly!! Crazy obsessions with eye liner!! And just who is Robert, the Dreaded Phylum Porifera!!!

Please Note: We offer large and small cast versions of this play. Cast and royalty numbers for both are below.

Cast Size: 45/13 Flexible M-F Roles Doubling Possible.

Royalties: $50.00 per performance.

Running Time: Approximately 120/45 Minutes.

"May the Dwarf be with you in this wacky take on the classic fairy tale which will have audiences rolling in the floor with laughter!

What happens when you mix an articulate mirror, a conceited queen, a prince dressed in purple, seven little people with personality issues, a basket of kumquats and a little Star Wars for good measure?

Cast Size: 12 Flexible M-F Roles.

Royalty: $50.00 per performance.

Running Time: Approximately 45 Minutes.

"My dreams of thee flow softly.
They enter with tender rush.
The still soft sound which echoes,
When I lower the lid and flush."

They say that porcelain is the best antenna for creativity. At least that's what this cast of young people believe in Dear John: An ode to the potty! The action of this one act play takes place almost entirely behind the doors of five bathroom stalls. This short comedy is dedicated to all those term papers, funny pages and Charles Dickens' novels that have been read behind closed (stall) doors!

Cast Size: 10 5M 5F.

Royalties: $35.00 per performance.

Running Time: Approximately 15 Minutes.

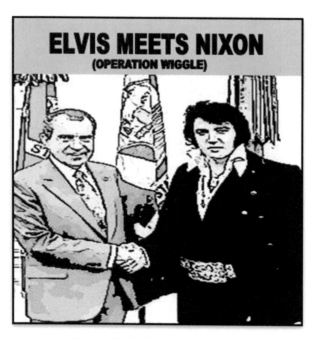

Declassified after 40 years!

On December 21, 1970, an impromptu meeting took place between the King of Rock and Roll and the Leader of the Free World.

Elvis Meets Nixon (Operation Wiggle) is a short comedy which offers one possible (and ultimately ridiculous) explanation of what happened during that meeting.

Cast Size: 2 M with 1 Offstage F Voice.

Royalties: $35.00 per performance.

Running Time: Approximately 10 Minutes.

In the beginning, there was a man.
Then there was a woman.
And then there was this piece of fruit...
...and that's when everything went horribly wrong!
Even Adam is a short comedy exploring the relationship
between men and women right from day one.

Why doesn't he ever bring her flowers like he used to?
Why doesn't she laugh at his jokes anymore?
And just who is that guy in the red suit?
And how did she convince him to eat that fruit, anyway?

Cast Size: 3 2M-1F.

Royalties: $35.00 per performance.

Running Time: Approximately 10 Minutes.

Count Dracula is bored. He's pretty much sucked Transylvania dry, and he's looking for a new challenge. So it's off to New York, New York! The Big Apple! The town that never sleeps...that'll pose a challenge for sure. Dracula purchases The Carfax Theatre and decides to put on a big, flashy Broadway show!

Cast Size: 50 Flexible M/F roles with Doubling Possible.

Royalties: $50.00 per performance.

Running Time: Approximately 90 Minutes.

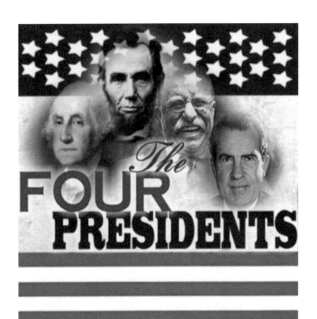

THE FOUR PRESIDENTS is an educational play which examines the lives and characters of four of the most colorful personalities to hold the office. George Washington, Abraham Lincoln, Theodore Roosevelt and Richard Nixon. Much of the dialogue comes from the Presidents' own words.

A perfect show for schools!

Cast Size: 10 Flexible M-F Roles with Doubling Possible.

Royalties: $50.00 per performance.

Running Time: Approximately 60 Minutes.

The lights rise on a beautiful sunset.
A mermaid is silhouetted against an ocean backdrop.
Hauntingly familiar music fills the air.
Then...the Lawyer shows up.
And that's when the fun really begins!

It's The Little Mermaid (More or Less.)

Cast Size: 30 Flexible M-F Roles with Doubling Possible.

Royalties: $50.00 per performance.

Running Time: Approximately 45 Minutes.

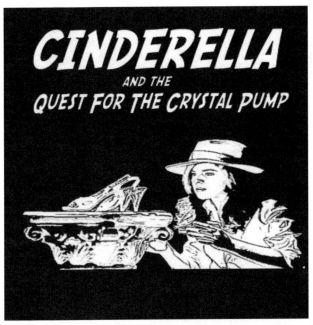

Cinderella and the Quest for the Crystal Pump, is the story of a young girl seeking a life beyond the endless chores heaped upon her by her grouchy stepmother and two stepsisters. But more than anything, Cinderella wants to go to the prince's masquerade ball, but there's one problem...she has nothing to wear! Luckily, her Fairy Godperson has a few ideas.

Please Note: This play is available in large and small cast versions. Both cast sizes and royalty rates are listed below.

Cast Size: 30/13 Flexible M-F Roles with Some Doubling Possible.

Royalties: $50.00 per performance.

Running Time: Approximately 90/45 Minutes.

Shorespeare is loosely based on a Midsummer Night's Dream. Shakespeare, with the help of Cupid, has landed at the Jersey Shore. Cupid inspires him to write a play about two New Jersey sweethearts, Cleo and Toni. Shakespeare is put off by their accent and way of talking, but decides to send the two teenagers on a course of true love. Toni and Cleo are determined to get married right after they graduate from high school, but in order to do so they must pass this course of true love that Cupid's pixies create and manipulate. As they travel along the boardwalk at the Jersey Shore, Cleo and Toni, meet a handful of historical figures disguised as the carnies. Confucius teaches Cleo the "Zen of Snoring", Charles Ponzi teaches them the importance of "White Lies", Leonardo Da Vinci shows them the "Art of Multitasking", and finally they meet Napoleon who tries to help them to "Accept Shortcomings" of each other. After going through all these lessons, the sweethearts decide that marriage should wait, and Cupid is proud of Shakespeare who has finally reached out to the modern youth.

Everyone has heard the phrase, "it's the squeaky wheel that gets the oil," but how many people know the Back-story? The story begins in a kingdom far, far away over the rainbow – a kingdom called Spokend. This kingdom of wheels is a happy one for the gods have blessed the tiny hamlet with plentiful sunshine, water and most important –oil. Until a terrible drought starts to dry up all the oil supplies. What is to be done?

The powerful barons of industry and politicians decide to hold a meeting to decide how to solve the situation. Since Spokend is a democracy all the citizens come to the meeting but their voices are ignored – especially the voice of one of the poorer citizens of the community suffering from a squeak that can only be cured with oil, Spare Wheel and his wife Fifth Wheel. Despite Spare Wheel's desperate pleas for oil, he is ignored and sent home without any help or consideration.

Without oil, Spare Wheel's squeak becomes so bad he loses his job and his family starts to suffer when his sick leave and unemployment benefits run out. What is he to do? Spare Wheel and Fifth Wheel develop a scheme that uses the squeak to their advantage against the town magistrate Big Wheel who finally relents and gives over the oil. Thus, for years after in the town of Spokend citizens in need of help are told "It's the squeaky wheel that gets the oil."

Once upon a time, a beautiful princess was placed under a magic spell by an evil fairy. A spell that would cause her to fall into a deep, deep sleep. A sleep from which she would awaken 1000 years later.

It's "Sleeping Beauty meets Buck Rogers" in this play for young audiences.

Royalties: $50.00 per performance.

Cast Size: 13 with flexible extras.

Running Time: Approximately 45 minutes.

Santa Claus. Frosty. Rudolph. Jack Frost.

This Christmas…if you've got a problem and if you can find them then maybe you can hire…THE SLEIGH TEAM!!!

The team is hired by lowly clerk, Bob Crachit to help his boss, the miserly old Ebenezer Scrooge find a little "Christmas Spirit"!

Royalties: $50.00 per performance.

Cast Size: 6

Running Time: Approximately 45 minutes.

The Odd Princesses is a parody/mash-up that opens with a group of princesses assembled for a card game in the palace of the notoriously messy Snow White. Late to arrive to the party is the perpetually neat Cinderella who has run away from home after becoming fed up with being treated like a maid by her stepmother. With no where else to turn, the two total opposites decide to move in together! What could go wrong?

Royalties: $50.00 per performance.

Cast Size: 8 with extras possible.

Running Time: Approximately 45 minutes.

Eager to escape the clutches of the Big Bad Wolf once and for all, the Three Little Pigs build a time machine and travel back in time 150 million years to the Jurassic era where they quickly discover they have problems much bigger than the Big Bad Wolf. Much, much, much bigger!!!

Royalties $35.00 per performance.

Cast Size: 6+ extras with flexible M-F roles.

Running Time: Approximately 30 minutes.

Dr. Victor "Vickie" Frankenstein has just inherited his grandfather's castle in foggy Transylvania...but what secrets lie in the ultra-secret, subterranean laboratory located beneath the castle??? It's a little bit monster story and a little bit Rock and Roll!

Royalties $50.00 per performance.

Cast Size: 16. 8 principle roles, 8+ Extras possible.

Running Time: Approximately one hour.

Made in the USA
Columbia, SC
19 December 2023